My Hamster's A Genius

A play by Dave Lowe

ORiGiN™
Theatrical

FOR ALL ENQUIRIES CONTACT: ORiGiN™ Theatrical
PO BOX Q1235, QVB Post Office, Sydney, NSW, 1230, Australia
Phone: (61 2) 8514 5201 Fax: (61 2) 9299 2920
enquiries@originmusic.com.au   www.origintheatrical.com.au
Part of the ORiGiN™ Music Group
An Australian Independent Music Company

should not be considered to be necessarily endorsing or otherwise attempting to promote an affiliation with any of the owners of the brand names or trademarks or public figures. Such references are solely for use in a dramatic context.

LANGUAGE NOTE

Licensees are welcome to make small alterations to the language that is used is this play so as to make it suitable for a younger cast and/or audience.

MUSIC USE NOTE

Licensees are solely responsible for obtaining formal written permission from copyright owners to use copyrighted music in the performance of this play and are strongly cautioned to do so. If no such permission is obtained by the licensee, then the licensee must use only original music that the licensee owns and controls. Licensees are solely responsible and liable for all music clearances and shall indemnify the copyright owners of the play(s) and their licensing agent, ORiGiN™ Theatrical, against any costs, expenses, losses and liabilities arising from the use of music by licensees. Please contact the appropriate music licensing authority in your territory for the rights to any incidental music. In Australia and New Zealand, contact APRA AMCOS apraamcos.com.au.

If you are in any doubt about any of the above then contact ORiGiN™ Theatrical.

For complete listing of plays and musicals available to perform and all licence enquiries, contact ORiGiN™ Theatrical.

www.origintheatrical.com.au
+ 61 2 8514 5201

AND HERE ARE THE RULES
IN PLAIN ENGLISH FOR YOU...

AUTHOR – DAVE LOWE

Dave Lowe is a Brisbane-based children's author, playwright and writer for TV, with books published in the UK and Australia, and translated into six languages. The 'Stinky & Jinks' series, of which 'My Hamster is a Genius' is the first book, has sold over 150,000 copies worldwide.

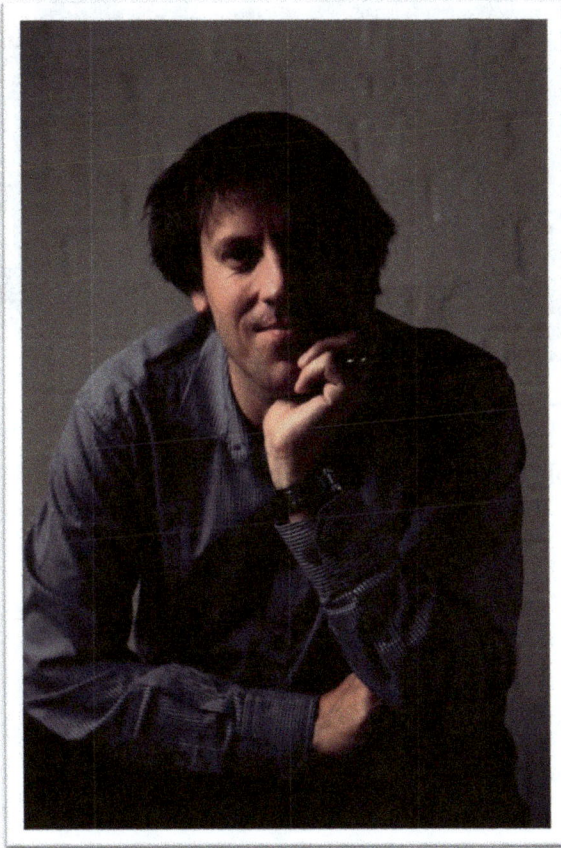

Premiere Production: Brisbane Arts Theatre August 2019.

Cast: Isaac Cain, Jeremy Hauter, Edie George Chambers, Tia Reynolds, Oliver Martin, Courtney Farrar, Emile Regano, Steve Durber, Rachael McFarlane, Szonja Meszaros.
Directed by John Boyce
Photography by Nick O'Sullivan

Cover design by Sean Dowling

CHARACTERS

Ben (11, but should be played by an older kid/adult)

Lucy (9, ditto)

Tyson (11, ditto)

Mum

Dad

Beardy McCreedy

Stinky (puppet, though the puppeteer is visible whenever Stinky is on stage)

Sasha / Extra student

O'Malley

3rd Penguin / Meerkat

Police officer

The stage is split between Ben's small bedroom and the rest of the stage, where all the other action (Lucy's performances, the scenes inside and outside school) take place. The only room in Ben's house we ever see, however, is Ben's room: all other action in the house is off-stage.

ACT ONE

SCENE ONE

We're in BEN's bedroom – it's pretty messy. There's a desk and a chair and a single bed – on which (sticky-taped to it, in fact) is BEN's little sister, LUCY. BEN faces the audience.

BEN   Never – never sticky-tape your little sister to your bed: even if she asks you to. I did, and my mum is about to go absolutely bananas. She has a long history of unusual punishments. Once, when she caught me giving Lucy's Barbie doll a haircut – she sat *me* down and cut *my* hair in the same style…

MUM enters. LUCY is wriggling but apparently not able to get free.

MUM   *(Almost speechless)* What…? Why…?

BEN   She asked me to. Tell her, Luce.

LUCY wriggles some more.

MUM   Right, Ben. The last straw. That's it – I'm… I'm buying you a pet!

BEN   *(Expecting a severe punishment)* No, Mum! Anything but… – wait, what?

MUM   I'm taking away all your things…

1

(She picks up toys from the floor and then the X-Box)

BEN   Please! No! Not the X-Box...!

MUM   For you, Benjamin, it's an *ex*-X-box...

LUCY   Good one, Mum.

MUM   *(To BEN)* ...You're eleven years old, for heaven's sake! You'll only get all this back when you show me you can take care of something other than yourself!

LUCY   Hello? I'm stuck here! I'm literally stuck to the bed!

MUM   Ben – release your sister.

MUM storms out – BEN untapes LUCY, who runs out, blowing him a raspberry. BEN, alone in his room, deflated, takes a piece of paper, sits at his desk, and writes out a list.

BEN   *(To himself)* Now – what pet to get?

SCENE TWO

It's later that day. BEN is in his bedroom. MUM enters, followed by DAD and LUCY (who is now wearing a penguin costume). BEN stares at LUCY.

BEN   Lucy?

LUCY   It's for the new show – 'Cheerful Feet'…

DAD   They couldn't get the rights to 'Happy Feet'.

LUCY   Mum's doing the costumes again – I'm trying it
            for size. I'm 'penguin on the left'. Sasha Collins
            got middle penguin. Sasha – again! (*To MUM*)
            So, about the pet, Mum – I was wondering, can
            we get a…?

MUM   A penguin? In Brisbane? Of course not.

LUCY   I was going to say 'unicorn'.

MUM   They don't exist, Lucy.

LUCY   Ponies exist.

MUM   (*Looking around the room*) And where would Ben
            keep a pony – in his socks-and-pants drawer?

DAD   What about a greyhound? 'Cos I know a bloke
            from the TAB who…

MUM   No, Derek.

BEN hands MUM the list.

BEN   Just a few ideas.

MUM   (*Reading*) Octopus?

BEN   We'd obviously need a swimming pool too…

MUM   Husky dog?

BEN   And a pair of rollerblades, so I wouldn't have to walk to school anymore.

MUM   Platypus? Monkey? Bumble bee? No, Ben. Anyway, I've already been to the pet shop. (*She leaves and comes back in with the cage containing STINKY. The cage is proportionate to the size of the hamster. There's a little house and a wheel.*) Da-dah!

BEN   What is it?

MUM   A hamster.

MUM places the cage on the desk.

BEN   Does it do anything?

DAD   (*Sarcastically*) Yes, it tap-dances, juggles and plays the ukulele. (*Beat*) I imagine it sleeps a lot, eats a lot and poos a lot.

LUCY   Can we call her Chloe?

MUM   No – because it's a boy.

DAD   How do you know?

MUM   How do you think?

DAD lifts the hamster out of its cage and inspects the hamster's undercarriage.

DAD   It must be very small. His – umm – you
             know…his doodle. (*He puts the hamster back.*)
             How about calling him 'Winx' – like the
             racehorse? Or Black Caviar? *Brown* Caviar? Phar
             Lap? *Fur* Lap?

BEN   Wait – if he's my pet – and I have to look after
             him…

MUM   You most certainly do.

BEN   …then can't I call him whatever I want?

LUCY   Not fair – it's a punishment pet, remember!

MUM looks at DAD, who shrugs.

MUM   So, Ben – what are you going to call him?

BEN gives this a lot of thought.

BEN   Jasper Stinkybottom!

LUCY giggles. MUM and DAD sigh etc. LUCY, MUM and DAD exit.

SCENE THREE

It's later. BEN is sitting on his bed, bored. STINKY is asleep.

BEN   Nothing to do. And my new pet – snoring his tiny head off. I might have to resort to – (*grimaces – in mock horror*) my *homework*. (*He takes out his books.*) Maths. Question One. (*Scratches his head.*) Eighty-five minus twenty-eight. Eighty-five minus twenty-eight.

STINKY   (*Mildly irritated*) Fifty-seven.

BEN   (*Mumbles*) Fifty-seven.

BEN writes this down, moves onto Question Two.

BEN   One hundred and twelve minus seventy-four.

STINKY   Thirty-eight.

BEN   Thirty-eight. Thanks.

BEN writes this down too – then pauses, startled. He shakes his head – he must have imagined it.

BEN   Ninety-three minus sixty-five.

STINKY   Twenty-eight.

BEN jumps up, flustered, looks around – under his bed, in a cupboard, outside the door.

BEN   (*On edge*) Ninety-three minus…

STINKY   For goodness sake! It's twenty-eight.

BEN looks around, even more flustered, before staring at the hamster, wide-eyed.

            It's rude to stare.

BEN points at him, speechless.

            Also, it's rude to point.

BEN   (*Astonished*) Not *you*?

STINKY looks behind him, as if there might be another talking hamster around.

STINKY   I don't see anyone else here.

BEN   You know how to…?

STINKY   Do very basic maths?

BEN   I was going to say 'talk'.

STINKY   I can hear things too as it happens. Like your dad discussing my…

BEN   (*Blushing*) Sorry.

STINKY   And 'Jasper Stinkybottom'? Really? How would
              you like it if you were called – for example –
              'Roger Smellington' or 'Sebastian Poo-Poo'?

BEN   Not much – especially not 'Sebastian Poo-Poo'.
              Sebastian's a terrible name.

STINKY   But what's done is done I suppose – you may call
              me 'Stinky'.

BEN   I'm Ben. High five!

STINKY stares at him.

STINKY   Hamsters only have four fingers.

BEN   High four!

STINKY sighs.

STINKY   Ben – you couldn't get me *out* of here, could you?

BEN   Sure.

He takes Stinky out of the cage and puts him on the desk.

STINKY   Careful – I'm not a toy, you know. So – you're
              not very good at maths, I take it?

BEN   Or spelling. Or art. Or anything really.

STINKY   From what little I've seen of you so far, you seem
            to have a real talent for nose-picking. You can
            even get your *thumb* up there. It's quite
            impressive really. Twenty-eight.

BEN   Sorry?

STINKY   The answer to your question.

BEN   Oh. Right. Thanks. (*He sits down and writes.*) I
            need to show the working-out too, if you don't
            mind. Otherwise Beardy McCreedy will think I
            used a calculator. He's very suspicious like that.

STINKY   Beardy McCreedy?

BEN   My teacher – he's got this enormous beard – you
            could hide a medium-sized possum in it. And he
            hates kids. I've got Japanese homework for
            tomorrow too. Don't suppose you speak Japanese,
            do you?

STINKY   Hamusutaa ni shite wa, watashi no nihongo umai
            desu yo.

BEN   Sorry?

STINKY   I said, 'My Japanese isn't bad, for a hamster'.

Spotlight on BEN, who is addressing the audience.

BEN   When you have a genius hamster in your room,
               you really don't need an X-Box anymore. I rush
               home from school each day to hang out with him.
               He helps me with my homework – okay, who am
               I kidding? – he *does* my homework, in return for
               a steady supply of carrots.

BEN turns to STINKY, who is sleeping.

               I'm home, buddy. (*STINKY doesn't wake.*)
               English homework today – *Describe your house
               in detail.*

BEN sighs. No answer from STINKY.

               Stinky? I'm home! (*Increasingly concerned*) Are
               you okay? (*To audience*) Maybe I killed him with
               too much homework. Is that even a thing? I
               always told Mum it might kill me. Stinky?! Are
               you – dead?

STINKY   I wish.

BEN is hugely relieved.

BEN   Oh, thank goodness.

STINKY   I am trying to sleep.

BEN   Sorry.

STINKY   'Unkempt', by the way.

BEN	Pardon?
STINKY	It means 'messy'. *Describe your house.* The homework. Your room, like your hair, is 'unkempt'.
BEN	Oh. Nice word. How do you spell that?
STINKY	Later. I'm going back to sleep. I was dreaming about carrots.
BEN	You're always asleep.
STINKY	I'm crepuscular, in case you hadn't noticed.
BEN	Crep-what?
STINKY	Crepuscular. It means we're active at dawn and dusk – you know, like kangaroos. Basically, we need an afternoon nap. Which you are currently disturbing – yet again…
MUM	(*Off-stage, yelling*) You did what?! What on earth were you thinking?
STINKY	…and if it's it not *you* disturbing my sleep, it's your sister's incessant tap-dancing, like someone's knocking at the door but never coming in – or it's your mum, who really doesn't seem to have an 'inside voice'.

MUM	(*Off-stage, loudly*) No – of course – you *weren't* thinking, Derek! As usual!
BEN	It's just Dad in trouble again. Nothing for us to worry...

MUM bursts in, followed by a sheepish DAD.

MUM	Tell him, Derek.
DAD	Well, where to start...?
MUM	(*Impatiently*) Is anyone helping you with your homework, Ben?
BEN	Nope. No *person* is helping me with my homework. No, Mum. I swear on Lucy's life.
MUM	Good, because your father has made a really stupid bet.
DAD	I bumped into your teacher at the TAB. Herbert McCreedy. I went to school with him. Mum too. He had a crush on Mum...
MUM	He's only human.
DAD	Barely. He was just the same, even back then. No beard, obviously. But the same absolute...
MUM	Derek.

DAD	And he said to me in the TAB today, he said – 'your son's homework has been consistently excellent these past few weeks'. And I said – 'brilliant'. And he said – 'oh, it's not a compliment: the boy is obviously cheating'. And I said, 'How dare you?' Or words to that effect. And then he said – 'The apple never falls far from the tree'…
BEN	Apples? Trees?
DAD	That's exactly what *I* said. Apparently, it means…
MUM	It means, kids always turn out like their parents.
BEN	Is that true? (*Looks at MUM and DAD*) Say it's not true, Mum.
MUM	It's not true.
BEN	Phew.
MUM	But instead of walking away from Mr McCreedy, like an actual grown-up might have done…
DAD	I made a bet.
BEN	Oh?
DAD	He's giving you a maths test in class tomorrow…
BEN	What?!

DAD   …and if you pass, he'll dye his beard bright pink.

BEN chuckles, then frowns.

BEN   And, if I don't…

DAD   Then we'll have to wash his car. You and I.

BEN   Phew. Because I was worried it was going to be
               something…

DAD   Wash his car with toothbrushes.

BEN   What?

DAD   In front of the school. In outfits of his choosing.
               But – look, you haven't been cheating – so there's
               absolutely nothing to worry about. Good lad.

MUM and DAD leave. MUM apologetically, DAD sheepish.
STINKY looks at BEN.

STINKY   Why are you so calm? Even someone as smart as
               I am can't teach an idiot like you mathematics in
               just one evening.

BEN   You don't need to. I've got a brilliant plan.

SCENE FOUR

We're in the hall outside BEN's classroom. BEN is sitting with a lunchbox on his lap (holes have been poked into the lid. STINKY is inside it. The puppeteer is on-stage but BEN is addressing the lunchbox). BEN is anxious, fidgety.

STINKY   Even by your standards, this is a completely terrible idea. It smells of old sandwiches in here…

BEN   It's nearly time, Stinky.

STINKY   and it's very dark…

BEN   So, have a nap.

STINKY   It's impossible to sleep when you're constantly being jiggled around…

BEN   Sorry – I'm a bit nervous.

STINKY   *You're* nervous? How would you like to be trapped in a lunchbox all day?

BEN   I wouldn't.

STINKY   Though it's hardly much worse than being at home in my prison.

BEN   We've discussed this, Stinky. It's called a 'cage'. Not a prison.

STINKY	How would you like to sleep twenty-seven centimetres from your own poo…?
BEN	Not much.
STINKY	It's been three days since you cleaned it out – and the newspaper that's currently lining it is *The Sunday Mail*, for goodness sake. And, even worse, the *sports* section! One thing you need to know about rodents, Ben, is that we're not even slightly interested in rugby league.
BEN	You don't *have* to be in the cage. I'd really miss you, but I've offered – loads of times, now – to release you into the wild…
STINKY	Do you have any idea what would happen to me in the wild? Do you know which animals like to eat hamsters? Practically all of them. Cats, birds, dogs… I'd be a furry little snack within minutes…
BEN	Look – the bell's about to go. I'll pop you – gently – into my shirt pocket, you'll whisper the answers to me, and then we'll go home to a freshly-cleaned cage and as many delicious carrots as you can eat…

We hear TYSON approaching.

It's Tyson – the horrible kid in my class I was telling you about.

TYSON   *(from off-stage)* Benjamin Jinks.

STINKY   He's *eleven*? He's got a very deep voice.

BEN   He's been kept back a few years. Now – shush.

TYSON enters, swaggers over to BEN and grins broadly when he sees the lunchbox.

TYSON   And they say that there's no such thing as a free lunch. What you got in there for me?

BEN   Nothing. It's totally empty.

The following happens in slow-motion: TYSON distracts BEN, takes off the lid. STINKY leaps out, bites him on the finger.

TYSON   Ow! Ow! Ow!

STINKY scurries off stage. BEN jumps up. TYSON is hopping in pain.

               I'll get you for this!

TYSON searches for STINKY, but gives up.

               And when I get hold of that rat I'll wring its neck!

TYSON stomps off, holding his finger.

               Seriously: *Ow!*

BEN   Stinky. Stinky! (*He gets on all fours, searching frantically.*) It's safe. There's no one here. Quick!

He can't find the hamster. BEARDY enters.

BEN   He's gone, Stinky. Come here, boy!

BEN notices BEARDY.

BEARDY   Jinks!

BEN   Sir?

BEN stands up.

BEARDY   What are you looking for down there? Your brain?

BEN   No, sir.

BEARDY   Because – I hate to tell you – that may be a lost cause.

The bell rings. BEARDY rubs his hands together.

Ah – showtime! I parked the BMW under a tree today – the tree was full of cockatoos. Cockatoo poo – an absolute a devil to clean. Come on, boy – this way. (*He shoos BEN into class and addresses the audience*). They say revenge is a dish best served cold – and I've been waiting thirty years to humiliate my one-time nemesis, Derek Jinks.

SCENE FIVE

MUM is tidying BEN's room. STINKY isn't there. As she talks, she's making the bed, picking up clothes from the floor etc.

MUM   Hiya, Stinky.

She looks in his cage but she can't see him.

You must be curled up in that little house of yours, snug as a bug. Don't blame ya, mate. Sorry about your name, by the way. I'm not too happy with Brenda, to be honest. This room, honestly: I'll tell you something – you're the lowest maintenance one in this family, by a long way. Lucy, I love her, but – my goodness she's whiny. (*She impersonates Lucy:*) 'Mum, Ben just…' 'Mum, I need a…' 'Mum, Sasha's mum lets her…'

And as for my son – your owner – bone-idle. I mean, look at the state of this room – it's a pig-sty. A guinea-pig sty, *you* might call it. Get it? And as for Derek – it's just like having three kids. Sometime I'm not even sure why I… Ah, you don't need to hear this. So, this is what it's come to, using a rodent as a psychologist. Sometimes, with this family, though, it's just nice to talk to someone who can't answer back. (*She looks at her watch.*)

Right – I've gotta pay the electricity bill, then off to the supermarket. Somehow squeeze in two hours of work. Take Lucy to dance class. Sometimes, you know, *I'd* like to be the one dancing. I had all the moves, back in the day. (*She does a dance move as she tidies.*) I used to shake it like a polaroid picture. (*She waggles her bum rhythmically at the cage/the audience.*) See?

Where was I? Lucy's dance class. Right. Then home to cook dinner. Ben will probably pull a face. (*Impersonation of Ben:*) 'Broccoli? Yuck. Broccoli looks like a cartoon fart.'

You know, Stinky, sometimes it feels like I'm running on a wheel too: always on the go but never actually getting anywhere.

She signs and exits with an armful of dirty clothes.

SCENE SIX

We're in class. TYSON – finger bandaged – is at the desk next to BEN, scowling at him. Two other STUDENTS are also in class – one is O'MALLEY (but it's implied that it's a full and noisy class).

BEARDY   (*To class*) Settle down! Settle down!

(*STUDENTS are holding noses etc – someone has farted.*)

(*He winces*) Oh, for crying out loud – that smells like one of yours, O'Malley. Put a cork in it, son. (*To the class*) Settle down! (*They settle down*) Just one more hour of this torture to get through – then we can all go home and do things we actually like. Oy! Quiet reading time – books open, mouths shut.

I said 'mouths shut, O'Malley. I'm sure if you really put your mind to it, you could breathe with your mouth closed. It's called 'Evolution'. Tyson – *book* –

TYSON is reading the book upside-down. BEARDY turns it around.

Just look at the pictures.

Jinks here has a special test – so we can find out once and for all if, as I strongly suspect, he's a sneaky little cheat, like his father. (*He slams the test paper onto BEN's desk.*) Clock's ticking, son.

We hear the clock ticking. BEARDY, feet up on his desk, is reading the form guide while occasionally checking on BEN. TYSON is occasionally glaring at BEN and making threatening gestures. Ben is obviously struggling with the test – flitting between trying to answer by himself and looking around the classroom for STINKY. Eventually – the implication is that quite a lot of time has passed – BEN spots STINKY in the corner of the room. When nobody is looking, BEN beckons the hamster over. STINKY navigates an assault course, around table-legs, chair-legs, schoolbags, feet etc, until he reaches BEN, who leans forward to scoop him up. But…

BEARDY   Jinks! Will you sit up straight!

When BEN thinks that nobody is watching, he leans forward again. TYSON sees this (but doesn't see the hamster on the floor). He points to BEN.

TYSON   Mr McCreedy.

BEARDY   Jinks!

BEN sits up. TYSON and BEARDY are now both keeping a close eye on him. So STINKY makes a decision – to climb up inside BEN's trouser leg. The puppeteer moves discreetly away.

BEN   (*Whispering*) Stinky! Not up the trousers! Ow!

BEARDY   Boy!

BEN   Cramp, sir. My calf. (*To STINKY, whispering*) That's my thigh, Stinky. Be careful up there – very careful. (*He jumps up*) Yeeooww!

BEARDY   Boy! Do you have ants in your pants?!

BEN   Not ants, sir.

STINKY is now climbing up inside BEN's shirt. BEN winces.

22

(*Whispers, pleading*) Careful with the nipples, Stinky. Right – I'll tell you when the coast is clear.

BEN is waiting for the moment when both TYSON and BEARDY are distracted. (O'MALLEY knocks something heavy off the desk.)

O'MALLEY   Sorry!

TYSON and BEARDY look over to O'MALLEY.

BEN   (*Whispers*) Now.

We seem to go into slow-motion. Eg O'MALLEY picks up the book in slow-motion. Perhaps the clock can tick in slow motion too. With assistance from the puppeteer, STINKY leaps out from inside the shirt, does a double-somersault and lands in BEN's pocket.

               (*Whispers*) Right – quick. Question One.

STINKY, however, is now fast asleep and snoring. Nothing that BEN can do – prodding, whispering – can wake the hamster up.

The bell rings. BEN leaves disconsolately, avoiding TYSON. O'MALLEY trips. BEARDY picks up BEN's test paper and reads through it – a broad grin spreads across his face, which turns into a satisfied chuckle.

SCENE SEVEN

*We're in BEN's bedroom. We see that he's got his things back –
X-Box, toys etc. BEN is wearing a bright T-shirt with, in big
letters, I AM A CHEAT. He has a bucket and a toothbrush and is
glaring at STINKY*

STINKY   I told you I was crepuscular.

*DAD enters. He's wearing a tutu and a T-shirt with 'Like father,
like son' on it. He also has a bucket and a toothbrush.*

DAD   *(With a sigh)* Come on, son. A bet's a bet.

MUM and LUCY enter. DAD and BEN are surprised.

MUM   We're coming, too.

BEN   To laugh at us?

MUM   To support you. That's what families do, Ben.
                Through thick and thin. Or, in our case, through
                thick and thick.

LUCY nods, then waggles her head, equivocating.

LUCY   I might accidentally laugh a bit.

They all leave.

*The following action takes place beside BEARDY's car (which is
off-stage), and in BEN's bedroom – the focus switches between*

the two. Beside BEARDY's car we see MUM, LUCY, BEARDY, TYSON and a couple of STUDENTS. It's implied that they're all watching BEN and DAD clean the car. (O'MALLEY might be taking selfies with BEN and DAD in the background. TYSON has a schoolbag – when he sees that the entire Jinks family is there, he slips away.

BEARDY   And there are people who say that teaching isn't a rewarding profession. Still think you made the right choice, Brenda, all those years ago?

MUM   Oh, yes. He looks great in a tutu. Cracking legs. You were never my type, Herbert.

BEARDY   Luxury car. Luxuriant beard. Long holidays. Your loss. (*To DAD, shouts*) Missed a bit, Derek! Put your back into it, old man!

BEN's bedroom. TYSON enters. He's robbing the house. His large schoolbag is now full of things stolen from other rooms. He takes the X-Box and stuffs it into the bag. He is about to leave when he notices STINKY in the cage.

TYSON   You. I'm gonna wring yer scrawny neck. (*He inserts a hand into the cage. STINKY bites it. TYSON withdraws his hand, hopping and yelping.*) Right. That's it. You're dead… (*He's about to insert his hand into the cage again when his phone goes. He answers it.*) I'm in the middle of – oh. On their way? Right. (*He hangs up. Points at STINKY.*) Lucky. Very lucky.

*TYSON slips out of the bedroom. MUM, DAD, BEN and LUCY
arrive home from their car-washing ordeal but are off-stage (ie
not in Ben's bedroom). STINKY (and the puppeteer) are reacting
with growing impatience to how slowly the penny is dropping for
them.*

MUM   Ben, did *you* leave that window open?

BEN   No.

MUM   Lucy?

LUCY   It was probably Ben.

BEN   No it...

MUM   Maybe it was me, letting a bit of fresh air in.

BEN   Did someone move the computer?

LUCY   Not me.

MUM   Who left that drawer open?

DAD   Crumbs! We've been burgled!

We hear footsteps – they're all running to investigate.

LUCY   My I-pad!

MUM   My jewellery!

26

BEN bursts into his bedroom.

BEN   My X-Box! No! (Pause) Stinky! You're safe!

STINKY   That's the order of importance, is it? Right…

BEN   No – I just…

STINKY   I know who it was. The burglar.

BEN   You know the…?

STINKY   Tyson.

BEN takes a while to comprehend this.

BEN   But – what…? Why…? How…? I'll call the police and tell them…

STINKY   Tell them what? 'My hamster can identify the thief'? If anyone finds out I can talk – even your own family – I'll be taken away and have experiments performed upon me. Rodents in science labs, Ben – it never ends well…

BEN   Right. So…?

STINKY   He received a phone call, right here – a call that just about saved my life. He has an accomplice.

BEN   A what?

STINKY	A helper. Someone who is clearly the brains of the outfit.
BEN	Right. So…?
STINKY	So someone needs to follow Tyson, after school – like a spy. See where he goes, what he does, who he meets…
BEN	And you'd be willing to *do* that? You said you never wanted to go outside again…
STINKY	I'm not talking about *me* Ben – I'm talking about *you*.

SCENE EIGHT

It's Cheerful Feet, the musical. LUCY and two dancers (one of whom – the one in the middle – is LUCY's nemesis, SASHA) do a tap-dance routine. LUCY keeps trying to get in the limelight, but SASHA keeps (subtly) pushing her out. LUCY gets more and more frustrated – she finally gets to the front when the music stops, but SASHA steps in front of LUCY as they take their bows.

SCENE NINE

The action is split between Ben's bedroom (STINKY is in the cage, with a walkie-talkie) and the school grounds, where BEN is hiding behind a tree, spying on TYSON, who is leaning against a wall, looking shifty. BEN talks to STINKY by walkie-talkie.

BEN   He hates school – but he's still here, twenty-five
             minutes after the final bell? It doesn't make sense.
             Plus, I think it's going to rain.

STINKY   Yes – a ninety percent probability.

BEN   How do *you* know that?

STINKY   We animals just know these things. Dogs, birds,
             hamsters – we can all sense when a storm's
             coming – I get a tingle in my fur.

BEN   Really?

STINKY   No. I just read it right here, you dingbat, because
             you lined my prison…

BEN   Cage.

STINKY   …with the weather-and-horoscope page of
             yesterday's newspaper.

BEN   I thought that being a spy might be fun – it *seems*
             fun, in the movies – but in real-life it's actually
             half terrifying, half really boring.

STINKY   *You're* bored?! I've been stuck here all day as
             usual with absolutely nothing to do.

BEN   You've got a wheel.

STINKY	(*Sarcastically*) Woo-hoo! Going round and round all day and getting absolutely nowhere. Brilliant! And – the *horoscope* section? 'Scorpio – today's your lucky day.' No it isn't. 'You'll make an important new friend...' No, I won't – 'and discover new horizons' – not while I'm stuck in here I won't. Plus, your little sister will be back at any moment: and when *you're* not around, she sneaks in here and dresses me up in her dolls' clothes. And *you're* talking about a combination of boredom and terror? You should try being me for a...
BEN	Shh. I think someone's coming.
STINKY	Right. Take photographs. Evidence.
BEN	Will do. Over and out.

BEARDY walks over to TYSON, who hands him the bag of stolen things. BEARDY hands TYSON a document folder and some money. BEN snaps a photo and ducks back behind the tree. But the flash goes. BEARDY and TYSON react.

BEARDY	What was that?
TYSON	Dunno. I'll check it out.

TYSON walks purposefully over to BEN'S tree. The lights go out.

END OF ACT ONE

ACT TWO

SCENE ONE

We pick up just before we left off: BEN takes the photo, the flash goes off:

BEARDY   What was that?

TYSON   Dunno. I'll check it out.

TYSON walks over to BEN'S tree. As he's one step away, there's a flash of lightning, followed quickly by a rumble of thunder.

BEARDY   (*Shouts*) It's just a storm. Let's get out of here.

BEARDY walks off. TYSON hurries off in the other direction – past BEN's tree, but thankfully doesn't look back. BEN slumps in relief. There's the sound of heavy rain. BEN leaves.

SCENE TWO

In Ben's room, LUCY enters, checking that BEN isn't home. She's holding a Barbie and some dolls' clothes. She takes STINKY out of the cage – shaking her head, baffled, at the walkie-talkie. She dresses STINKY up and does a role-play between Barbie (who is Lucy) and STINKY (who is given the role of Sasha). STINKY doesn't speak, however – LUCY does both voices – like a bad actor.

BARBIE   Hi, Sasha.

STINKY   Hi, Lucy, how are you?

BARBIE   I'm fine thanks. What about you?

STINKY   Well, funny you should ask. I've just realised that I'm really not good at dancing and I'm actually a bit of a big-head. Also, I'm very spoilt. And I think you should take the lead role in the next show.

BARBIE   Me? Oh, I absolutely couldn't.

STINKY   But you completely deserve it, Lucy – you're a brilliant dancer and a really nice person. Modest, too.

BARBIE   (*With false modesty that continues throughout 'Sasha's' compliments*) Ah, you're just saying that.

STINKY   And you're really pretty…

BARBIE   Ah, thank you, but I'm really not.

STINKY   …Like a young Ariana Grande.

BARBIE   Oh, you…

STINKY   Everyone says so.

BARBIE   Oh no, I'm absolutely sure they d… Who says so?

STINKY   Everyone. Lilah, Layla, Leela, Lola – everyone.

BARBIE   Well, if you're completely certain.

BEN enters, wet.

BEN   Lucy?! We've talked about this. Put him down.
                Stinky doesn't like dress-ups.

LUCY   Is it raining?

BEN   (*Sarcastically*) No, I just had a shower in my
                clothes.

BEN carefully takes STINKY off LUCY.

LUCY   How do you know he doesn't like dress-ups? He's
                always got the same look on his face. Like this:

She does an impression of STINKY.

                (*Teasing*) And I hear you talking to him, you
                know – you put on this funny voice so it's like
                he's talking back. Weirdo.

BEN   Out!

LUCY exits with her Barbie.

LUCY   Mum, Ben's a weirdo!

MUM   (*Off-stage*) I know, dear!

STINKY   Can you take this thing off?

BEN   But that dress really suits you, Stinky.

STINKY glares at him. BEN takes the dress off.

STINKY   Get caught in the rain, did you?

BEN glares at him. Then remembers that he hasn't yet reported back.

BEN   You'll never guess who Tyson was meeting.

STINKY   Your teacher, Beardy McCreedy.

BEN   It was... (*Surprised*) Yeah, how did you know?

STINKY   I put two and two together. (*Pause.*) It's four, by the way.

BEN   You're like a rodent Sherlock Holmes. *Fur*lock Holmes.

BEN is pleased with the joke. STINKY sighs.

           How did you work it out?

STINKY   Firstly, there was the homework: 'Describe your house in detail'? He was gathering information.

BEN   Today's homework is actually 'Your most valuable possession'.

STINKY   Exactly. And he'd be able to find out everyone's
            address from the school computer system.
            Secondly – you aren't the only family in your
            class to be burgled. I heard your mum saying that
            the O'Malleys were broken into, last week. And,
            finally, how many teachers do you know who
            have a new BMW? They're not *that* well-paid, are
            they?

BEN   Beardy – a criminal mastermind!

STINKY   But he won't be a match for *one particular* mind.

BEN   (Points to his own brain). *This one?*

STINKY gives him a look.

            Oh.

STINKY   It's time to do your homework, Ben.

BEN   This is no time for homework.

STINKY   'Your most valuable possession'. And, isn't Lucy
            in another show next week?

BEN   Yeah. 'The Tiger Queen' - they couldn't get the
            rights to The Lion King. Instead of 'Circle of
            Life', they've got a song called 'Square of
            Existence'.

STINKY	So, we set a trap. We'll tell Beardy about something valuable that Tyson missed the first time, and let him know when the house will be empty... I'll dictate it to you, if you like.
BEN	No, Stinky. I realised something, as I was cleaning Beardy's car: I need to do my own work from now on.

BEN takes out his exercise book and writes as he says the following:

	'Next Friday night, we are all going out to the theatre' – wait, how do you spell 'theatre'?
STINKY	T.H.E.A.T.R.E.
BEN	Thanks.
STINKY	You're welcome.
BEN	'...to watch my sister perform – she wants to wear Mum's diamond necklace. But Mum says it's much too valuable...'
STINKY	V.A.L.U.A.B.L.E.
BEN	Thanks. You're like a furry little spellcheck. 'It's sticky-taped under my bed, to keep it safe. So Lucy will go to the show, which starts at 7pm, without the necklace.'

STINKY   (Surprised) Nice job. Now – nap time.

STINKY starts snoring immediately. A tap-tapping sound comes from off-stage and he wakes.

                I wish he'd stolen those tap-shoes.

BEN   I'll go ask her to be quiet.

BEN leaves. DAD enters, sits on the bed and addresses STINKY, awkwardly.

DAD   Hi Stinky. My mate, Russell Jackson – he's got a
                Jack Russell, called Jack. Russell, my mate,
                confides in Jack – the Jack Russell – when they
                go for long walks – Russell says it's really
                therapeutic: you know, talking things through
                with Jack – the Jack Russell. And I know you've
                only got a pea-sized brain, Stinky, but – here
                goes…

                So, I'm giving up betting. After the Herbert
                McCreedy incident. It's got to stop. I'm still in the
                doghouse with Brenda. And I can't say I blame
                her. I just want to make it up to her somehow.
                Was thinking of writing her a song – what do you
                think? Actually, more like a rap. I've always
                secretly wanted to be a rapper.

DAD picks up a cap that BEN has left on the floor and puts it on backwards.

'Yo, Brenda.' What rhymes with Brenda? Lender? Mender? 'Yo Brenda – you mix me up like a food-blender.' Or what about: 'Yo Brenda, you're my favourite person of the female gender'? Oh, that's good. 'For you, I'm giving up betting.' Hmm. What rhymes with 'betting'? Forgetting? (*Loudly*) Heavy petting?

As DAD is saying 'heavy petting', BEN walks in.

BEN   (*Surprised*) Hi Dad.

DAD   (*Embarrassed.*) Son. Just checking your room was tidy. And it's not. Well done.

DAD takes cap off, places it on the bed, and exits.

BEN   What?

STINKY   You really don't want to know. (*Pause*) Have you ever considered putting a lock on your door?

SCENE THREE

It's next Friday evening. BEN is in bed, faking illness. LUCY comes in, dressed as a giraffe, followed by MUM and DAD.

BEN   (*Croaking*) Giraffe?

LUCY   Sasha Collins is the 'Tiger Queen'. Sasha, Sasha, Sasha. Cinderella? Sasha. Who was an ugly sister? Me, that's who…

BEN   Well…

LUCY   Who was Snow White?

DAD   Sasha?

LUCY   Yes. Who was 'Dopey?'

DAD   You.

LUCY   Correct.

DAD   (*This has been troubling him for a while.*) I don't
             remember a giraffe in The Lion King.

MUM and LUCY glare at him.

             What?

BEN   I just wish I was well enough…

DAD   (*Too enthusiastically*) I can stay and look after
             him, if you like.

MUM   No, Derek.

BEN   I'm fine. I mean, not fine. But I just need to rest in
             peace. Not 'Rest in Peace'. I mean, just – have a
             bit of peace and quiet.

DAD   But…

MUM	We've discussed this, Derek. Ben's proved he can be responsible now. I trust him to stay home alone for an hour or so and not get into trouble...
BEN	Thanks, Mum.
MUM	(*To DAD*) Leave him your phone, like we agreed, and he'll call if there's a problem. Won't you, Ben?
BEN	Yes, Mum. (*To LUCY*) Break a leg.
LUCY	I will. *Sasha's* leg.
MUM	*Lucy.*
LUCY	Joke. (*Mouths to audience*) I really will.

MUM, DAD and LUCY all leave.

STINKY	Let's do it. Thumbtacks.

BEN sprinkles them under the bed.

STINKY	Walkie-talkies.
BEN	Check.
STINKY	Phone, to call the police.
BEN	Check. (*He takes STINKY out of the cage and places him on the desk – then picks up one of the*

walkie-talkies and the phone and is about to leave, when he stops.) Are you sure about this, Stinky? You're putting yourself in great danger.

STINKY   When you spend your life in an eleven-year-old's bedroom, locked in a – cage… you have to take any opportunity for a bit of excitement. And those two villains need to be stopped.

BEN cuddles STINKY.

Careful – there's a very fine line between a hug and a throttle, you know.

BEN   Sorry. (*He takes another look at STINKY.*) You look twitchy.

STINKY   I'm a hamster. We twitch. That's what we do. You, on the other hand, look incredibly worried.

BEN   I'm a human. We worry. That's what we do. (*Pause.*) Good luck, then, Stinky. I'll be in the shed, waiting for your signal.

STINKY   Lightbulb out.

BEN stands on the chair, untwists the lightbulb.

SCENE FOUR

LUCY (Giraffe), SASHA (Tiger) and other kid (Meerkat) tap-dancing to 'The Square of Existence' (a bit like 'Circle of Life'). LUCY is again manoeuvred to the outer by SASHA, though this time, in doing so, SASHA twists her ankle (it's not LUCY's fault) and LUCY is super-excited to be centre-stage for the finale. Then they take their bows and stand to the side of the stage.

ANNOUNCEMENT (*off-stage*):   We finish this show with a special presentation to our long-time costume supervisor, Brenda Jinks, to be made by her husband Derek. Come up and take a bow, Brenda.

MUM is in the audience. She gets up, embarrassed and walks onto the stage. DAD walks onto the stage wearing a cap and holding a bunch of flowers. He hands her the flowers. In his other hand, behind his back, is a microphone. LUCY is mortified.

DAD   This goes out to my sweet, sweet, Brenda.

He turns the cap so it's on backwards.

LUCY   Please, Dad. Not rapping – not in public.

DAD   Yo, Brenda Jinks
             Everybody thinks
             You're absolutely great – including me.

You make all the costumes and you don't charge a fee
(except for the materials, which is completely understandable).
You're 'sew' amazing. That's 'S.E.W.' so –
Without your creations, there would never be a show.
Brenda, you're smart, you're strong and super-funny,
You're creative, you're kind and you're really good with money –
The opposite of me. But from now on, you see,
I'm never gonna go to the TAB.
I'll never, ever gamble, never be in debt
'Cos you, my darling Brenda, you are my winning bet.
So this goes out to the incredible Brenda.
You're a force of nature, a wonderful friend, a brilliant mum.
You've got a really cute…

LUCY   Dad!

DAD   And you don't have to be a fortune-teller
To see that you and me are a winning quinella.
Brenda Jinks, you're a spectacular wife.
Yo, Brenda – you're the best thing in my life!

LUCY   (*Having had enough embarrassment*) Dad!

DAD   But now it's time for me to stop.
Thanks everybody. Mic drop!

DAD does a mic-drop. LUCY, despite herself, laughs. MUM hugs DAD. The MEERKAT leads SASHA limping off.

SCENE FIVE

STINKY is in the bedroom. BEN is in the shed, pacing, shivering, with the walkie-talkie.

BEN	Anything happening?
STINKY	Not yet. How's the shed?
BEN	Colder than a polar bear's bum. Ah – a costume from Cheerful Feet. That should keep me warm.
STINKY	Here *I* am, about to come face-to-face with a boy who has already threatened to kill me – twice – and you're complaining about the *cold*.
BEN	It's okay for you – you've got fur. You probably don't know what it's like to be cold. It's like you live your entire life wearing a cute little hamster onesie. Adorable.

BEN spots some of the costumes his mum made for previous shows. He puts down the walkie-talkie and puts on a penguin costume.

STINKY	'Adorable?' 'Cute'? I'll have you know, these teeth are sharp like razors. I'm a lean, mean biting machine. These claws of mine, like tiny knives.

You should see the damage I can do to a carrot. I'll slice it, I'll dice it, I'll…julienne it…

STINKY does some martial arts moves, with 'Miss Piggy' karate noises.

They call me the carrot-y kid.

BEN is now in the penguin costume and has picked up the walkie-talkie.

BEN   (*To STINKY, Patronisingly*) Ah, bless.

BEN looks around. He sees a box of his old toys. He takes out a Slinky, a whoopee cushion, a fake dog poo etc.

I was wondering where all this stuff went.

STINKY   (*On the walkie-talkie, urgently*) I can hear something.

BEN is lost in reminiscing and doesn't seem to hear STINKY. He pulls out a water-pistol – in a certain light, it could just about pass for a gun.

This water pistol - always guaranteed to make Lucy mad. Great times.

STINKY   I can hear something!

We hear someone breaking in.

45

Call the police, Ben.

BEN uses the walkie-talkie.

BEN   Right. (*Pause.*) What's the...?

STINKY   Triple zero.

BEN   Right. I knew that.

STINKY   And don't use the walkie-talkie from now.

BEN   Right.

STINKY   Like, from *now*.

BEN   (*Into walkie-talkie.*) Got it. No walkie-talkie.
                 (*Realises*) Sorry. Over and out.

*BEN puts down the walkie-talkie, but he can still hear what's
happening with STINKY. BEN tries to use the phone but it's not
easy, with the flippers of the penguin costume getting in the way.
He fumbles the phone, bends to pick it up, topples over, finds it
hard to get up again.*

*Meanwhile, TYSON enters the bedroom. It's dark. He flicks the
light switch but the light doesn't come on, so he uses the torch on
his phone instead. Crawls under the bed.*

TYSON   Ow! Ow! Ouch! Ow!

He gropes around for the diamond, but eventually realises it's not there. He crawls out.

Ouch! Aarghh!

He stands up, shines the torch around the room. Focuses on the cage. Lifts the roof off the house.

Where's the rat?

In the shed, BEN, finally calls the police.

BEN   Police. Yes. A burglary at 15 Palm Road, Spring Hill. Yes – now. Right now. Hurry!

Back in the bedroom, TYSON glimpses STINKY on the desk.

TYSON   A-ha. There you are. It won't have been a complete waste of time if I get to squish you…

STINKY leaps off the desk, scurries around the bedroom. TYSON chases after him for a while, until he has STINKY cornered. He reaches out.

TYSON   I've got you now, you little…

STINKY   Step away, brute – or I'll bite your hand off.

TYSON   It spoke! It spoke?

TYSON slaps himself.

STINKY   I'll do more than speak, dimwit, if you don't
                scram.

TYSON   (*Gibbering*) A – a talking rat.

STINKY   Hamster. I'm a hamster, you numbskull. And –
                what is more – I know everything, Tyson.
                Everything.

TYSON   You know my name?

STINKY   And all about your nefarious scheme – you and
                that hairy teacher.

TYSON is shocked. Then he calms down.

TYSON   Wait. In case you hadn't noticed, I'm about ten
                times bigger than ya.

STINKY   And about a hundred times dumber.

TYSON   Yeah. Well – you know too much. So – bye-bye
                rat.

*TYSON is about to squish STINKY. BEN picks up the water-
pistol, dashes out of the shed, and bursts into the bedroom.*

BEN   (*Deep voice*) Step away from the rat!

STINKY   Hamster.

BEN   Hamster.

TYSON   Aaah! A talking penguin!

BEN   I'll do more than talk if you don't leave my friend
             alone. Hands up!

TYSON   A penguin? In Brisbane? With a gun? What's
             happening to me?

*He runs from the bedroom, arms in the air. We see the flashing
blue light and hear the siren followed by the clink of handcuffs.*

POLICE   You're under arrest. You have the right to remain
             silent...

TYSON   I'll tell you everything! Just get those crazy
             talking animals away from me!

*We hear a car pull up. It's MUM, DAD and LUCY. The car door
opens.*

MUM   What on earth?

DAD   Huh?

LUCY   Tyson?!

TYSON   Aaah! A talking giraffe!

*In BEN's room, BEN quickly tidies up the thumbtacks, replaces
the lightbulb, stuffs the penguin costume under the bed, puts
STINKY back in the cage and is now lying in bed, trying to look
sick.*

SCENE SIX

BEN is now sitting up in bed, STINKY in the cage, MUM sitting next to BEN on the bed, DAD and LUCY are hovering. They're all in a state of shock.

MUM   I'm never, ever leaving you alone again – not until you're at least twenty-one.

BEN   I'm fine, Mum.

MUM   Twenty-two. Honestly, I'd never have forgiven myself.

She hugs him, very tightly.

BEN   There's a fine line between a hug and a throttle, Mum.

DAD   (*Puzzled, in 'Columbo' mode*) So, you were lying in bed when the burglar burst in…?

BEN   Correct.

DAD   And he was so shocked to see you that he ran off? And immediately confessed? It's a boy from your class? Herbert McCreedy is behind the whole thing? Which, I must say, is not as surprising as you might think, knowing the man. Probably feeding his gambling habit…

MUM shoots DAD a look.

SCENE SEVEN

BEARDY, wearing a hat, is pursued by the POLICE OFFICER. There's a chance for a bit of slapstick – it ends with his arrest. The POLICE OFFICER whips the hat off.

POLICE   It'll take more than a disguise to escape the law.

She attempts to tug his beard off.

BEARDY   Ow! It's real! It's real!

The beard comes off.

Oh. (He sighs, knowing that the game is up. Shrugs.) At least in prison, I won't have to teach kids anymore.

SCENE EIGHT

In the bedroom, everyone is where we left them. LUCY is scanning the room, like a detective in a TV show.

LUCY   What's the penguin costume doing here?

BEN   I like dressing up as penguins.

LUCY   And the water pistol? And the walkie-talkie? It doesn't make sense?

MUM   It really doesn't.

BEN gets out of bed and addresses the audience. (The family doesn't acknowledge this.)

BEN   It wears you out, doesn't it? Telling fibs. You tell a tiny little lie, and then you need to tell another lie to cover up the first lie, and then a slightly bigger lie, and before long there's a penguin costume under your bed...

He sits back on the bed, next to MUM and, after taking a deep breath, addresses her and DAD.

            The truth is, we set a trap for the burglar tonight.

DAD   You – you set a trap?

MUM   We?

BEN   Me and my hamster.

MUM   You – and...?

BEN   Stinky here. He's an actual genius.

MUM   And you know he's a genius because...?

BEN   He talks.

DAD   In English?

BEN   And Japanese actually. Come on, Stinky. Say something.

Everyone stares at the cage. STINKY doesn't respond. They all look back at BEN.

MUM   Derek, call the home doctor.

BEN   No, no, Mum. I'm okay. Really. I can explain. It was like this – I was in the shed in the penguin costume, and Stinky was telling me what was happening – on the walkie-talkie.

MUM   There, there, Ben. Mummy's here. It'll be okay. You've just had a nasty fright, that's all. A burglar in the house – it's enough to give anyone a shock.

BEN   I'm telling the truth, Mum. Honest. Tell them, Stinky. Say something… (*He looks at Stinky, imploringly*) He must be traumatised…

DAD   *Someone's* definitely traumatised.

BEN   Stinky! Tell them!

MUM hugs BEN.

DAD   I'm calling the doc.

BEN   Okay – sorry. Mum's right. Maybe I just need to rest.

DAD sighs with relief. MUM hugs him tighter.

DAD   Good lad. Come on, Lucy – let's give your
                brother some space.

*LUCY is not convinced, but leaves with DAD. MUM tucks BEN
in and strokes his head. Then she leaves the room. BEN waits
until he's sure no one can hear, then sits up.*

BEN   Thanks a lot, Stinky. Now they all think I've gone
                bananas.

STINKY   You must have. Why else would you tell them
                about me? Do you really think they're capable of
                keeping a secret? Your sister would tell the whole
                school in five minutes flat and I'd be in all the
                newspapers and on the TV and scientists would
                take me away and…

BEN   All right, all right. Calm down.

They glare at each other, until:

                We did it though, Stinky – didn't we?

STINKY   We did. We certainly did. High four.

They high five each other.

SCENE NINE

*We're in BEN's room a week later – BEN's not in, but STINKY is
in the cage. MUM comes in with a carrot, singing tunelessly*

54

(making up the song as she goes) and wiggling, latin dance style. She's clearly in a great mood. STINKY (via the puppeteer) is traumatised by the content of MUM's song. She initially uses the carrot as a microphone, then puts it in the cage and goes on to tidy the room.

MUM   (Singing) Hey, Stinky, have a carrot!
                 Derek and I are doing latin dance together, twice a week!
                 Our marriage is back on track – he's got really good technique!

MUM exits, with dirty clothes. DAD enters, whistling contentedly.

DAD   (*To STINKY*) Just wanted to say thanks for listening the other day – it worked an absolute treat. I've actually been working on a follow-up rap…

Thankfully, from STINKY's point of view, DAD is interrupted before he can start – LUCY enters, wearing Sasha's tiger costume. DAD squeals in fright.

LUCY   It's just me, Dad – Lucy. Sasha unfortunately has to rest her ankle, so I'm the Tiger Queen now. Where's Ben? I wanted to show him.

DAD shrugs. They exit. BEN enters.

STINKY   We really need to talk about getting a lock on your door. How was your day?

BEN	Great. No Tyson, of course. My new teacher is brilliant: Miss Miles – she's funny and kind and a lot less hairy than the last one. Also, much less evil. How are you doing?
STINKY	Fine. I'm planning to spend a bit of quality time with the Carrot family, here. A bit of napping. Several poos.
BEN	Great.

BEN smiles. LUCY enters.

LUCY	Mum! Ben is talking to his hamster again.
MUM	(*Off-stage*) Lucy – be nice to your brother – he's been through a lot, remember.
BEN	Thanks, Mum!

LUCY pulls a face. She hovers in the room. She's clearly bored.

BEN	(*Not maliciously*) Fancy being sticky-taped to the bed again?
LUCY	(*Shrugs*) Sure.

STINKY looks at the audience and sighs.

STINKY	Here we go again.

THE END

GOSSAMER
John Misto

It began as an innocent game. In 1917, two young British girls experiment with a camera and capture images of themselves with dancing fairies. They are playing a joke – but no one is laughing.

Their photographs attract the attention of the two most famous men in the world – Sir Arthur Conan Doyle and Harry Houdini.

Here at last is proof that the spirit world exists. In an England devastated by World War 1, these fairy photos offer hope that a link to "the other side" is possible and that millions of grieving families can "contact" their lost sons.

What really happened at Cottingley Glen? Sixty years later an MI5 agent urgently needs to uncover the truth. However not all fairies are as kind as Tinker Bell, and he suddenly discovers that the bottom of the garden can be a dangerous place indeed.

"Gossamer unfolds like a mystery drama. Like the best mysteries it doesn't answer every question."
Mark Stoyich

"Misto is a master craftsman. He sustains his story's mystery and promise until the final blackout."
Sun Herald

Casting: 4M, 3F
Full Length Play, Drama, 1910s / WWI, 1970s

www.origintheatrical.com.au

HER HOLINESS
Melvyn Morrow and Justin Fleming

All Mary MacKillop wanted was to live the dream, but to others - the staunch hierarchy of the Roman Catholic Church - she was a nightmare.

What Mary MacKillop didn't count on was the degree of obstruction that would stand in her way - opposition from the very people whose sacred task it was to help her.

And for sure, St Mary MacKillop didn't expect to be humiliated and excommunicated, making it necessary for her to disguise herself and travel to Rome to confront the reigning pontiff, Pope Pius IX, in an attempt to brazen out the storm she endured over the years it took her to found and have recognised a religious order of women who would educate the young of wild and remote places in Australia.

Mary MacKillop was Australia's Martin Luther. The antipodean Thomas More. A woman for all seasons. But *her holiness* (the lower case is deliberate) takes this dramatic narrative in an unexpected direction.

"A confronting, moving and very entertaining piece of theatre"
Australian Stage

Casting: 11M, 6F
Full Length Play, Historical, Drama, Australian,
19th Century, 21st Century

www.origintheatrical.com.au

ORiGiN™
Theatrical

FOR ALL ENQUIRIES CONTACT: ORiGiN™ Theatrical
PO BOX Q1235, QVB Post Office, Sydney, NSW, 1230, Australia
Phone: (61 2) 8514 5201 Fax: (61 2) 9299 2920
enquiries@originmusic.com.au   www.origintheatrical.com.au
Part of the ORiGiN™ Music Group
An Australian Independent Music Company

www.ingramcontent.com/pod-product-compliance
Lightning Source LLC
Chambersburg PA
CBHW072211090426
42740CB00012B/2475